MEN-AT-ARMS SERIES

EDITOR: MARTIN WINDROW
ALBAN BOOK SERVICES

The American Provincial Corps 1775-1784

Text by PHILIP KATCHER

Colour plates by MICHAEL YOUENS

OSPREY PUBLISHING LIMITED

Published in 1973 by
Osprey Publishing Ltd, P.O. Box 25,
707 Oxford Road, Reading, Berkshire
© Copyright 1973 Osprey Publishing Limited

ISBN 0 85045 148 5

Printed in Great Britain by
Jarrold & Sons Ltd, Norwich

The Early Years

To say that policy concerning the raising and use of American Provincial troops was confused would be an understatement.

At first it was thought that the American rebels, a motley and untrained bunch of farmers with antique weapons, would flee in panic at the first sight of the red-coated might of King George III. Powder smoke rolling down over the corpses of Bunker Hill smothered that dream, and the British Army settled down to a new and unexpected role as besieged troops in Boston.

British officials remembered how long it had taken to train Provincial troops during the Seven Years War, locally called the 'French and Indian War', to the point where they were effective soldiers. Therefore Major-General Thomas Gage, commanding the army in Boston, decided initially to accept the offers of loyal subjects to form their own units only for militia duties.

'Garrison Orders, 29th October 1775. Some North British merchants residing here with their adherents having offered their services for the defense of the place, the Commander-in-Chief has order'd them to be armed and directed them to be formed into a company called "the Royal North British Volunteers". They will be distinguished by a blue bonnet with St. Andrews Cross upon it. Mr. James Anderson to be Captain, Wlm Blair and John Fleming, Lieutenants. The Guard Room and Alarm Post to be near Fennel Hall. The Company will mount a guard at

An officer and private of the Pennsylvania Loyalists – modern reconstructions of Provincial uniforms and accoutrements. The private wears the familiar red coat, tricorne and white small-clothes. His cartridge-box has a brass pierced insignia, the royal cipher, backed by a piece of red wool. His weapon is the Long Land model 'Brown Bess' musket. The officer, who holds a spontoon, wears a scarlet coat faced green and embroidered with gold metallic thread. He wears a gorget, a crimson silk sash and a sword; his hat is laced with gold thread, while the private's is bound with white linen. (The Pennsylvania Loyalists)

TEUCRO DUCE NIL DESPERANDOM.

First Battalion of PENNSYLVANIA LOYALISTS,
commanded by His Excellency Sir WILLIAM
HOWE, K. B.

ALL INTREPID ABLE-BODIED

HEROES.

WHO are willing to serve His MAJESTY KING
GEORGE the Third, in Defence of their
Country, Laws and Constitution, against the arbitrary
Usurpations of a tyrannical Congress, have now not
only an Opportunity of manifesting their Spirit, by
assisting in reducing to Obedience their too-long de-
luded Countrymen, but also of acquiring the polite
Accomplishments of a Soldier, by serving only two
Years, or during the present Rebellion in America.

Such spirited Fellows, who are willing to engage,
will be rewarded at the End of the War, besides their
Laurels, with 50 Acres of Land, where every gallant
Hero may retire, and enjoy his Bottle and Lass.

Each Volunteer will receive as a Bounty, FIVE
DOLLARS, besides Arms, Cloathing and Accoutrements, and every other Requisite proper to accommo-
date a Gentleman Soldier, by applying to Lieutenant
Colonel ALLEN, or at Captain KEARNY's Rendezvous, at PATRICK TONRY's, three Doors above
Market-street, in Second-street.

gunfiring and patrol the streets within a certain district and will take into custody any suspicious or disorderly persons found in the streets at improper hours.'

So read the first notice of Provincial units being formed and put to use by the British authorities.

After this notice came Timothy Ruggles's Loyal American Association, marked by the wearing of a white sash on the left arm; James Forrest's Loyal Irish Volunteers, marked by a white cockade, and Major Daniel Murray's red-coated Wentworth's Volunteers. These early units never reached regimental strength and, after the army abandoned Boston, the men went along to be merged into other, newly raised units. The leaving of Boston in fact meant that Americans serving the King would have to serve as more than mere militia thereafter.

With or without official British Army approval loyal Americans insisted on forming themselves into bands. In September 1775, during a militia field day in Maryland, half the Somerset County Militia put red cockades in their hats, flints in their muskets instead of the usual wooden snappers, and drove off the rebel half. Such spontaneous uprisings of loyal men did not always end well. The numerous Scottish Highlanders living in the backwoods of North Carolina formed into a loyal band and started on their way to the coast to join the Governor's forces. Not far from their goal, on 27 February 1776, they were met at the Widow Moore's Creek by a rebel militia band. The rebels had removed most of the planks of the bridge across the creek, but, undaunted, Captain Donald McLeod led his Highlanders to the attack. Scottish broadswords and muskets in hand, yelling their battle-cry, 'King George and Broadsword', the Highlanders scrambled across the bridge – only to be met by heavy volleys from rebel muskets. It was Culloden all over again. The sword-swinging Highlanders, stumbling across the damaged bridge, were no match for the steady rebel volleys. In less than a quarter of an hour the battle was over.

The rebels pursued and captured most of the Highlanders. Many of them ended up in Philadelphia's gaol, others changed loyalties quickly. This action damped for some time the general enthusiasm for forming loyal units in the south.

The Governor of Virginia, however, was forming units on his own. Besides a corps of escaped and freed slaves, Lord Dunmore authorized Lieutenant-Colonel James Ellegood to form a regiment known as the Queen's Loyal Virginia Regiment. Together with a regular regiment, the 14th Foot, this unit held a fort on the island of Great Bridge, Virginia. In December 1775 an overwhelming force of rebels attacked the two regiments. After a fierce little fight, involving charges back and forth into the fort and over the bridges connecting the island to either bank of the river, the royal troops withdrew. Lord Dunmore ended up a guest of the Royal Navy, within view of the land he was to govern, and the Queen's Loyal Virginia Regiment joined the main British Army.

That main army had, by now, decided to abandon Boston. Under miles of white sail, the army had set off for Halifax, Canada, to regroup and plan its strategy. Along with them went hundreds of His Majesty's loyal subjects. Meeting the fleet was one Archibald Campbell, who proposed to raise a Provincial regiment called the New York Volunteers. He had already raised two companies, but Major-General Sir William Howe, K.B., now in chief command, refused to equip them. 'It was not credited', wrote Provincial Muster Master Edward Winslow, 'that a General whose command was so extensive could possibly want the power to furnish common necessaries for 200 men, if his disposition toward them was favourable.' His initial disposition may have been unfavourable, but it must have changed for when the British Army left Halifax to storm the important city and harbour of New York, Campbell's two companies went with it.

The landings on Long Island, off New York City, went even better than could have been expected. The rebel army, now under General George Washington, had apparently hoped for another Bunker Hill, but Sir William was not to give them this pleasure. He hit them on the flank instead, and the rebel line folded like an accordion. On the left flank, under Major-General Grant, were the New York Volunteers who performed yeoman service.

Shortly after Long Island's fall, Sir William brought the army over to Manhattan Island,

Major Robert Rogers – as depicted in a mezzotint done in London in 1776. He was then commander of the Queen's Rangers, and it is possible that this uniform is the early one of that unit. (John Ross Robertson Collection, Metropolitan Toronto Central Library)

Finally realizing the potential of a Provincial corps, Sir William ordered 10,000 green coats faced white, blue and green, which were sent to him from England in December 1776. Later, as the corps grew more numerous, orange, black and buff facings were added. Waistcoats, breeches, hats, accoutrements and weapons were the same as the regular army issue, although in many cases the older types were given to Provincials. While the Short Land model 'Brown Bess' was the usual weapon of the regulars, the older Long Land model seems to have been used by many Provincial units.

While the number of units and men in the corps was growing, the way of loyal recruiters was far from easy. William Stone was shot to death for attempting to raise troops in Hartford, Connecticut. In fact that town, although heavily loyal, seems to have been a remarkably dangerous place to recruit. Moses Dunbar was later hanged there for the 'crime' of accepting a British commission and recruiting troops.

The typical commission for raising a regiment is worth looking at. Although dated rather later, the one issued by Sir William to another New Englander, Lieutenant-Colonel George Wrightman, is typical:

'You are hereby authorized and empowered to raise for His Majesty's service, a Regiment of able bodied men, to be composed of 30 Serjeants, 30 Corporals, Ten Drummers, and 500 Privates, divided into 10 Companies: each Company consisting of 1 Captain, 1 Lieut, 1 Ensign, 3 Serjeants, 3 Corporals, one drummer and 50 Privates, who will engage to cary arms under my orders, or the orders of the Commander in Chief of His Majesty's forces, for the time being, for two years, or if required during the continuance of the present Rebellion in North America: to receive the same pay, and be under the same discipline as His Majesty's Regular troops.

'The Officers are to be approved of by me, and their appointments by Commission, will depend on their success in Recruiting, they are to be instructed to raise the following numbers to entitle them thereto (vizt) a Captain, 30 men: a Lieut, 15 men; an Ensign, 12 men; and it is to be made known to them, that their pay will not commence until half the above number is raised,

again smashing into the rebel army on its flank. That island, too, fell rapidly. Then the major continental post of Fort Washington was taken and New York was firmly in British hands.

Now loyal Americans began flocking to the royal standard. Lieutenant-Colonel Robert Rogers, who had gained such fame in the Seven Years War with his rangers, began forming the King's Rangers, largely among Connecticut men. They seem to appear first in September 1776, when they were posted beyond the suburban New York town of New Rochelle. 'This corps', reported the Hessian Adjutant-General, 'as well as the New York and Grant's volunteer companies have repeatedly risked being fired upon, but since they resemble in many ways the rebels who have no uniform, the latter could not distinguish between friend and enemy.'

The uniform problem was soon to be solved.

and brought to the Rendezvous of the Recruits at Rhode Island.

'In like manner when one half the Corps is raised, mustered, and approved by a reviewing officer, a Major will be commissioned: and your Commission as a Lieut Colonel will be made out on 400 men being raised. In the meantime you will receive pay as a Captain until 250 men are raised: as Major until 400 are raised: and as Lieut Colonel from that period.

'Forty Shillings currency will be allowed as bounty for each man enlisted and approved.

'All officers civil and military, and others His Majesty's liege Subjects, are hereby required to be aiding and assisting unto you and all concerned in the Execution of the above service. For which this shall be to you and them a sufficient Warrant and Authority.'

One would like to report Colonel Wightman had good fortune in raising the Loyal New Englanders, as he called his regiment. Such, sadly, was not the case. On 28 July 1779 Muster Master Winslow reported to his New York headquarters:

'It is incumbent on me to observe that there is a corps called the Loyal New Englanders, commanded by Lieut Colonel Wightman, in which there are only fifty eight effectives, rank and file, altho. the warrant for raising this Corps has been granted above two years and officers have been appointed for three Companies – For some time past its number of men has been diminishing, and since I have resided at Newport, not a single recruit has been added to this Corps.

'From the most particular observations I am satisfied there is not the least probability of the number being increased or of his Majesty's service being benefited by the continuance of this Corps.

'I therefore humbly submit to you, whether it may or may not be expedient to recommend that the few men who remain may be drafted into some other Corps, and the officers seconded, as is usual in such cases.'

Such cases were indeed usual, especially among units raised early in the war. The Queen's Loyal Virginians, with their commander captured at Great Bridge, found themselves drafted into Rogers's unit. Rogers himself was found to be a poor recruiter, and his King's Rangers were renamed the Queen's Rangers as Rogers was replaced by Major Christopher French.

Yet, generally, recruiting went well in New York and eventually that colony provided 23,500 men to the Provincial Corps, mostly serving in the Westchester Refugees, the King's Royal Regiment of New York, Butler's Rangers, the King's Orange Rangers, the Loyal American Regiment, the Guides and Pioneers, the Queen's Rangers, the King's American Regiment, Jessup's Corps, and Delancy's Brigade.

A rifleman of the Queen's Rangers drawn by Captain Murray of that regiment. The black leather cap has a black-and-green feather attached at the cockade, and the short green jacket has small white shoulder-wings. The powder-horn was probably balanced by a bullet-bag worn on the left. There is no evidence of the sword which Simcoe states was issued to the riflemen. The trousers are white, gaitered. (John Ross Robertson Collection)

A grenadier of the Queen's Rangers. The fur cap also has a black-and-green feather, and the waistcoat is green. The coat, green faced green, has the 'winged lappets' seen in some British militia units and among Continental units. Apart from his belts, which are black, this soldier wears typical British grenadier accoutrements; although it is impossible to say if he is wearing a hanger.

A light infantryman and a hussar of the Queen's Rangers; both wear green jackets. The infantryman is in breeches and half-gaiters, the hussar in green trousers apparently worn over his boots. The hussar cap was adopted when a Hessian jäger shot a trooper wearing the earlier headgear, which dangerously resembled a Continental dragoon cap. (Both pictures from the John Ross Robertson Collection)

The latter unit was one of the first raised once the army had become settled in New York.

'Several times rebels have come into the English camp at night in small boats to join our army [the Hessian Adjutant-General reported]. They were assigned to Colonel Delancy's new brigade, which is now two thousand strong. The Colonel's ancestors settled on New York Island and he has suffered much from the rebels. Several hundred of the prisoners taken in the action of the 27th of August (Long Island Battle) have also been mustered into this brigade.'

Delancy's Brigade, which eventually numbered three battalions, was posted to Long Island for that island's defence. It seems that in their enthusiasm at recruiting a full brigade, just about anyone interested in joining was enlisted and, in early 1777, Colonel Delancy had to order that all Negroes and other 'improper persons' were to be discharged from the unit at once.

In addition, it was at New York that Brigadier-General Cortland Skinner raised his green-coated New Jersey Volunteers, which, with six battalions, became the largest Provincial regiment raised during the war. The King's Orange Rangers were raised in Orange County, N.Y. by 6 foot 2 inches tall, and 'proportionately stout', Captain John Coffin. The rebels offered $10,000 'for the head' of the leader of this mounted rifle corps. The men of the Loyal American Regiment and the Guides and Pioneers, who were mostly attached to that unit, were raised by Colonel Beverley Robinson from among the Scottish settlers who lived in the highlands above New York City. On the other hand, the King's Royal Regiment of New York, also known as Johnson's Royal Greens, was raised by Sir John Johnson on the Canadian–New York border where it served in frontier skirmishes. Walter Butler's famous Butler's Rangers usually served with them.

It was to Canada that the Continentals turned their attention now. They considered the country to be a 'fourteenth colony', and sent an invasion force under General Richard Montgomery to bring the Canadians into the fold. Montreal quickly fell and only weakly held Quebec remained. Quebec was held by a handful of regulars, six companies of English-speaking 'British' militia and eleven companies of French-speaking 'Canadian' militia. In September 1775 an artillery company was added to the militia. The men, clad in plain, lapel-less green coats and buff waistcoats and breeches, were reorganized into eight companies on the Continental Army's approach. The rebels attacked along the route taken by General James Wolfe years before, in a blinding snowstorm. The militia, supported by the few regulars, held on and broke up the rebel attack. The action ended, in fact, with the death of General Montgomery at the hands of some Canadian militia under Captain Francis Chabet. A relief column of regulars arrived in May 1776, and the militia was then disbanded. Canada had been saved and was never again so threatened.

A Policy Emerges

At last a definite plan concerning Provincial troops was being worked out. It was being recognized that merely arriving in a colonial city, raising the royal standard, recruiting and then hoping the Provincials could maintain law and order themselves, would not work. In April 1776 Sir Henry Clinton wrote:

''Tis clear to me that there does not exist in any one (colony) in America a number of friends of the government sufficient to defend themselves when the troops are withdrawn. The idea is chimerical, false, and if the measure is adopted . . . all the friends of government will be sacrificed en detail. This is the case in Georgia, will be in South Carolina, is already in North Carolina, in Virginia, will probably be in Boston, and must in my opinion be everywhere. If government are desirous that this experiment should be fairly tried anywhere, it must be in the provinces of Virginia and North Carolina conjointly. Such a disposition may be made as it will give it a fair trial, but if it succeeds the troops must not be recalled.'

The lessons of Moore's Creek and Great Bridge had been learned – at least in some quarters.

The army was in New York, however, and there it intended to stay. A militia was therefore raised to man the city's defences and free the regular and Provincial regiments to engage the Continental Army.

The *New York Gazette and Mercury* reported on 20 November 1777:

'The indulgences of the Commander-in-Chief has prompted the principal gentlemen, inhabitants of this city and refugees from other provinces, to form themselves into independent companies, twenty of which are nearly completed.

'Last Monday several companies of them paraded on the fields, at the upper end of Broadway, headed by the Worshipful David Matthews, Esq., and made a very fine appearance. These companies, together with the militia, will greatly add to the strength of the city, and relieve the King's troops, who may be employed elsewhere.'

As was often the case, however, the British High Command did not greatly respect the local militia. An officer of the 23rd Regiment of Foot wrote:

'One of the Battalions of this City Militia is commanded by Mr. David Mathews, the Mayor, and is Composed of Merchants and traders of New York. General Robertson, the Governor, having made them the present of a pair of Colours, they were out a few days ago to be reviewed by him, and some of the principal Officers, in describing what they could do, told him, they could, March, Wheel, form Columns, Retire, Advance & Charge. "Yes, Gentlemen,"

The Battalion (left) and King's Colours of the Queen's Rangers. They are of typical design, and measure 6 ft. × 6½ ft. The battalion colour is in the regimental facing colour – green. (John Ross Robertson Collection)

said the General, "I am convinced you can charge better than any other Corps in His Majesty's service."'

Militia, by all accounts, was the least useful type of Provincial unit raised. The Provincial Inspector-General, Lieutenant-Colonel Alexander Innes, wrote: 'I look upon it that every man intitled to serve in a provincial corps during the war is a useful soldier gain'd to the King's Service and I am well convinced the Militia on their present plan will ever prove a useless, disorderly, distructive banditti.'

With New York well in British hands, and Sir William and Washington playing cat and mouse in New Jersey, 1776 drew to an end. The new year promised, if everything went well, the war's end. Major-General John Burgoyne was to advance from Canada down through New York state to that city, cutting the southern colonies off from the more rebellious New England ones. Sir

William, at the same time, decided to take the rebels' capital, Philadelphia. These two moves, once accomplished, should crush the rebellion.

General Burgoyne's army was composed largely of regular and Brunswick troops, with only a handful of Provincials. Jessup's Corps, raised in New York by Major Ebenezer Jessup on the New York-Canadian border, was sent along with the expedition. At first the campaign went well. The rebel stronghold of Fort Ticonderoga fell quickly, and the army moved along on schedule. Soon, however, General Burgoyne discovered the vast American wilderness, which looked so easy to cross on the maps in his London club, was slow and tedious to penetrate. Trees had to be cut down and roads built for his wagons and artillery. The area was sparsely settled, and he failed to attract as many loyal subjects to join his army as he had expected.

One of his Brunswick regiments was a horseless

dragoon regiment. This, along with Jessup's Corps, was sent to Bennington, now in Vermont, where they hoped to find horses. They found, instead, rebel militia in overwhelming numbers, and the two units, after a fierce defence, were virtually destroyed. The men of Jessup's Corps here discovered for themselves how Provincial soldiers could expect to be treated by the rebels. One of them, half dead with his left eye smashed open by a musket-ball, was slung on a captured horse with a similar wound and led around for the amusement of the rebel militiamen. Other prisoners were ordered tied in pairs and attached by traces to horses, driven by Negroes. The state government ordered them to tramp their way through deep snows to make roads for the rebels to use – while clad only in thin shoes, or actually barefoot.

Burgoyne's main army was finally stalled at Saratoga, N.Y. There, after two battles at Freeman's Farm, short on supplies and surrounded on all sides by hostile militia, it was forced to surrender.

From New York, the city's commander, Major-General Sir Henry Clinton, led a diversionary attack on the posts of Fort Clinton and Montgomery, a short way up river. The move was an attempt to get the rebels to detach units from their northern army to go on the defensive around New York. While the diversion failed to reduce the pressure on Burgoyne, it was a classic

victory, and the force, consisting of some regulars, Emmerich's Chasseurs, the Loyal American Regiment, the Guides and Pioneers, the King's American Regiment, a company of the King's Orange Rangers, and the New York Volunteers, rapidly captured the two strongholds.

Capture of Philadelphia

The campaign against Philadelphia went equally well. Sir William had come south by sea, landing below the Pennsylvania city at the Head of Elk, Maryland. Among the other troops he had brought with him on this campaign were the Queen's Rangers and elements of the Loyal American Regiment and the Guides and Pioneers.

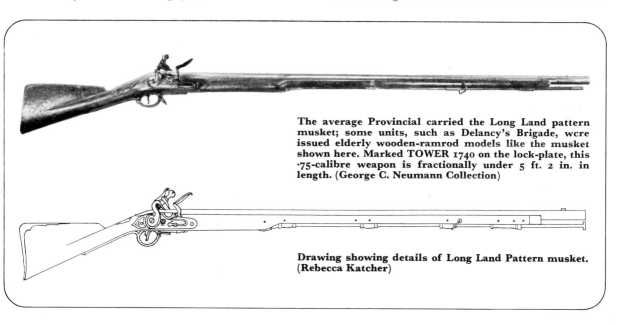

The average Provincial carried the Long Land pattern musket; some units, such as Delancy's Brigade, were issued elderly wooden-ramrod models like the musket shown here. Marked TOWER 1740 on the lock-plate, this ·75-calibre weapon is fractionally under 5 ft. 2 in. in length. (George C. Neumann Collection)

Drawing showing details of Long Land Pattern musket. (Rebecca Katcher)

John G. Simcoe, commander of the Queen's Rangers. Although probably of a later period, this portrait seems to illustrate the regimental uniform of the War of Independence period. (John Ross Robertson Collection)

They began their march north to the city. Washington had brought his main army south to defend his capital. On 16 September 1777 he drew up his army in defensive lines along the Brandywine Creek, with its centre on the ford of the main road to Philadelphia.

Again Sir William fooled Washington, displaying on his centre, but really swinging most of his army round the rebel's flank. Washington waited until, too late, he learned of the British flank manœuvre. Leaving his centre intact, he hurriedly sent in several regiments to hold off the British Army while he withdrew his battered men. At the ford facing the Continental centre the Queen's Rangers had been posted. While the guns of Proctor's Artillery Regiment fired on them from across the river, they stood their ground. Finally, much firing from the left was heard – Washington's flank had been turned – and the order to advance was shouted out. 'The Fourth Regiment led the column', wrote Queen's Rangers ensign Stephen Jarvis, 'and the Queen's Rangers followed, the (rebel) Battery playing upon us with grape shot which did much execution. The water took us up to our breasts and was much stained with blood before the battery was carried and the guns turned on the enemy.'

Washington's army was smashed, and fell back as fast as it could to reform. The Queen's Rangers added much glory to their reputation, but only at great cost. Fourteen officers lay dead or wounded as did a third of all the unit's other ranks. Although Washington again offered battle, a fierce rainstorm just before the action soaked weapons and cartridges, ending any chance for a fight. The way to Philadelphia was now open, and in September the Queen's Rangers were among the first troops to enter the city.

Pennsylvania had been one of the least rebellious cities in the colonies – besides being the second largest city in the English-speaking world at the time – and its subjects made fine recruits. Command of the Queen's Rangers passed to a regular officer, John Graves Simcoe, after its old commanding officer was wounded at Germantown during an abortive attempt by Washington to recapture the city. Simcoe immediately set about recruiting and rebuilding his command.

In addition, from the popular royalist feelings Sir William heard expressed, he confidently predicted a large number of Provincial troops would shortly be raised. On 21 October 1777 he wrote Lord Germaine in London: 'I am to request that additional clothing may be sent over for five thousand provincials, which, by including the new levies expected to be raised in this and neighbouring counties will certainly be wanting.'

Sir William's army recruited nothing like 5,000 men, but certainly they did do well in the city.

William Allen, Jnr, who had been a lieutenant-colonel in the rebel 2nd Pennsylvania Regiment, had resigned his commission upon hearing of the Declaration of Independence. He now set about raising the Pennsylvania Loyalists. This unit never had more than 200 men and, although it saw much service, the quality of recruits may not have been of the highest. On 11 May 1778 we find an advertisement in the *Pennsylvania Ledger*:

'Left at a house at the lower end of Third-street on Thursday the 7th inst. by a soldier belonging to the third regiment of Pennsylvania Loyalists, 18 pair of TROUSERS: if the person at whose house they are left will deliver them to the printer or have them brought to the London Coffee-house, shall receive ONE GUINEA reward and no questions asked.'

What sort of soldier would leave his company's trousers at some house which he couldn't find again, even though he knew the street, is certainly open to question.

James Chalmers, better known for his book *Plain Truth*, a rebuttal of Thomas Paine's inflammatory *Common Sense*, raised a sister battalion to the Pennsylvania Loyalists, the Maryland Loyalists.

Four dragoon companies were raised in the city: the Philadelphia Light Dragoons, under Captain Richard Hoveden; the Bucks County Dragoons, under Captain Thomas Stanford; James's Troop of Provincial dragoons, under Captain Jacob James; and the West Jersey Cavalry, under Lieutenant-Colonel John Van Dyke. These units were generally attached to other organizations, usually the Queen's Rangers, the British Legion or the King's American Dragoons.

Francis Lord Rawdon raised his Volunteers of Ireland, which was later taken on to the British establishment as the 105th Regiment of Foot. Sir William Cathcart formed the Caledonian Volunteers, which would eventually become the better-known British Legion. The Roman Catholic Volunteers, a corps which recruited among the city's many Irish, besides the Volunteers of Ireland, was organized by Alfred Clifton. Finally, Colonel Van Dyke also raised a foot unit, the West Jersey Volunteers.

Life in the liberated city was anything but dull, even though there were no major battles. The Pennsylvania Loyalists and the Roman Catholic Volunteers were called upon to assist with foraging expeditions across the Delaware River into rebel-held New Jersey. Other units constantly skirmished around the city's suburbs. A typical skirmish was fought 7 April 1778. Some forty Philadelphia

Contemporary engraving of Francis, Lord Rawdon, probably in the uniform of his Volunteers of Ireland. The 'brandenburgs' were common in Hessian regiments but rare among British or Provincial units. The small group of soldiers depicted below wear full gaiters and caps similar to those of the Queen's Rangers. They seem to have typical regimental coats, small-clothes and white belts. (New York Public Library)

Light Dragoons and fifty Bucks County Dragoons rode out of the city at dusk. They arrived near a rebel outpost near the suburban town of Frankford near midnight. While a rebel lieutenant and eighteen other ranks hid in the post, an old stone house, the rest of the rebels fell out into a battle line. Sabres glinting in the moonlight, the Provincial dragoons charged the rebels. One quick, scattered volley, and the line broke up, each rebel running for his life. Suddenly, however, the men hiding in the house poked their muskets through windows and doors, and opened fire on the dragoons' backs. Wheeling in line, the dragoons sped back to the house, surrounding it and capturing eight rebels. Nine other rebels lay dead in the moonlight. Not one Provincial was even wounded.

Another typical action involved the Queen's Rangers, some of the Philadelphia Light Dragoons, James's Troop of provincial Dragoons and some regular infantry and dragoons. The little brigade made its way up the Old York Road to the town of Billet where some 500 rebels had gathered. After making only a brief defence the rebels fled, leaving between fifty and sixty prisoners, eighty dead, and ten wagons full of much-needed military supplies. The whole British loss was two wounded.

After actions such as these the status of the Provincial Corps was changing. One sign of the inferiority of the Provincial soldier in the past had been his coat of green, while the regular soldier's coat was red. With the beginning of the 1778 campaign, however, it was decided to clothe Provincials in red coats, too.

Some Provincial troops, such as the Prince of Wales's American Regiment, had apparently been clad from the outset in red. Others were generally glad of the change, except Colonel Simcoe. He worked, successfully, to keep his corps in green, and to obtain green waistcoats, planning for the unit to wear the waistcoats, which had sleeves, during the summer's campaign, and the coats during the winter.

'Green', he wrote, 'is without comparison the best colour for light troops with dark accoutrements, and if it is put on in the spring, by autumn it nearly fades with the leaves, preserving its characteristics of being scarcely discernable at a

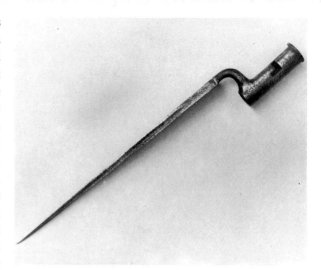

Socket bayonet for a 'Brown Bess' – the ultimate weapon in the hands of the British Army, including the Provincial Corps. (Author's collection)

distance.' The Philadelphia Light Dragoons, Bucks County Dragoons and James's Troop were ordered into green, too, so they could serve with the Queen's Rangers. Captain Stanford himself, however, seems to have favoured red, and wore it instead of green.

The Queen's Rangers, besides being active in local skirmishes, were active in recruiting. Many advertisements appeared in the three local papers calling for new members, and even a surgeon's mate, to come to the unit's Kensington headquarters. Simcoe reported:

'. . . the eleventh (company) was formed of Highlanders. Several of these brave men, who had been defeated in an attempt to join the army in North Carolina (at Moore's Creek), were now in the corps; to these others were added, and the command was given to Captain M'Kay; they were furnished with the Highland dress, and their national piper, and were posted on the left flank of the regiment, which consisted of eight companies, a grenadier and a light infantry company. [Later], Serjeant M'Pherson, a corporal and twelve men, were selected and placed under the command of Lieutenant Shaw; they were armed with swords and rifles; and, being daily exercised in the firing at objects, soon became the most admirable and useful marksmen.'

A hussar company was later added.

Sir William sailed from Philadelphia to England; Burgoyne's expedition had ended in disaster, and it was now up to the victor of Forts Clinton and Montgomery, Major-General Sir Henry Clinton, to create the final victory. He decided to concentrate the Royal Army in New York at first, and came down to Philadelphia personally to lead the troops through the Jerseys to New York. In June 1778, the army began its march. The Queen's Rangers were in the van along with the four dragoon companies; the Pennsylvania Loyalists moved along the flanks; the Roman Catholic Volunteers guarded the baggage; and the rest of the Provincials moved in the first division under Sir Henry.

Not far from Monmouth Court House at Freehold, New Jersey, the rebel army struck, initially by pure chance. The attackers at first were New Jersey militiamen, easily driven off by the Queen's Rangers. As the rebels ran, the scouts of the Queen's Rangers could see the main Continental Army, a single foot regiment in the lead. Into line, and straight ahead, bayonets levelled, the Queen's Rangers now pressed into this group. The winter's training at Valley Forge had proved its worth, however, and a single well-aimed rebel volley, together with four or five cannonballs, drove the green-coated men back.

The rebels, now formed into a single front, came on. While most of the British Army fell into defensive positions, the Queen's Rangers saw a chance on the rebels' left flank. They stormed across the fields towards that position, only to be met by heavy fire from all sides. Again they retired, and were then ordered to fall back to Freehold. The rebels had been unable to destroy any of the British Army or even stop its march. The British had been unable to destroy the rebel army. Both sides halted until, late that evening, the British Army resumed their march towards New York.

Once in New York, certain problems in the Provincial Corps had to be dealt with. Discipline in the Roman Catholic Volunteers had totally fallen apart. One man was court-martialled for advising a fellow soldier to desert to the enemy with his arms, accoutrements and equipment, and received a thousand lashes before being drummed

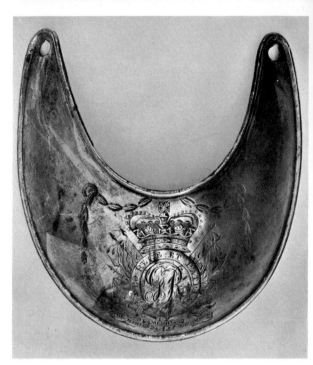

Officer's gorget marked with the regimental name, 'The King's American Regiment', and also with the number 4 for the alternative designation, '4th American Regiment'. Worn by officers on duty, the gorget hung round the neck on a ribbon of the facing colour, or attached by rosettes to the top coat collar buttons. (Metropolitan Museum of Art)

out of the service. Captain McKinnon, of that unit, was cashiered for 'ungentleman Like behavour', to wit, 'Plundering in the Jerseys', and 'suffering himself to be Kick'd by Capt McEvoy of the same corps on a Parade without properly resenting it'. McEvoy himself was cashiered for that kick, as well as 'taking a horse and cows' on the march from Philadelphia. Certainly no such corps was of much use to His Majesty, and the officers and men who remained were largely transferred to the Volunteers of Ireland.

Newport, Rhode Island, had been taken previously, and was now under siege. A relief column consisting of some regular regiments, elements of the Guides and Pioneers, The King's American Regiment and the Prince of Wales's American Regiment, were therefore sent to that city in June 1778. At the same time permission was granted to raise two units, the Loyal New Englanders and the Loyal Newport Associators. Despite French reinforcements and a large rebel force, the garrison there was able to hold on, and finally the siege was abandoned.

The year 1779 now rolled round, with troops well entrenched in New York, Canada and Newport, as well as the south. While the regulars went into winter quarters the Provincials and light troops remained active. In January a force of Delancy's Refugees and some of the Westchester Militia raided a grain and flour magazine three miles beyond White Plains, N.Y., bringing away the entire store loaded on thirty-seven wagons, as well as some captured militia officers. In the early spring a company of Delancy's Brigade raided some towns on the Connecticut shore equally successfully.

Such service was finally rewarded. On 2 May 1779 '. . . the Commander in Chief was pleased to signify, in general orders, to the Provincial troops, "that his Majesty, anxious to reward their faithful services, and spirited conduct, upon several occasions, has been pleased to confer on

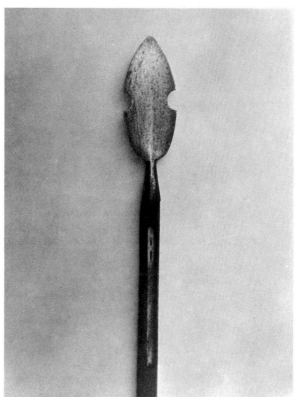

Officers carried spontoons as insignia of rank, as well as for more practical uses. Many had cross-bars. Being non-issue items, spontoons varied considerably throughout the Provincial Corps; this example has a head mounted on a black 6 ft. 7 in. staff. (Author's collection)

them the following marks of his Royal favour." The articles were then enumerated and all material to that service: the principal were: "That the officers of the Provincial corps shall rank as juniors of the rank to which they belong, and if disabled in service, should be entitled to the same gratuity as officers of the established army; and to distinguish the zeal of such regiments as will be completed, his Majesty will, upon the recommendation of the Commander in Chief, make the rank of those officers permanent in America and will allow them half-pay, upon the reduction of their regiments, in the same manner officers of the British reduced regiments are paid."'

This would be a major benefit to the Provincial Corps and its recruiting.

At the same time, the Queen's Rangers was taken on a new 'American establishment' as the 1st American Regiment, the Volunteers of Ireland as the 2nd American Regiment and the New York

Officer's sword-belt plate of the 4th Battalion, New Jersey Volunteers. (The New Brunswick Museum)

The standard white linen tent used by regulars and Provincials. This reconstruction, accommodating five privates, stands 5 ft. tall and 6 ft. square (Crisman Collection)

In June 1779 the Provincial regiments from Newport returned to New York and the corps was up to strength for its next campaign.

The War in the South

Volunteers as the 3rd American Regiment. Later, on 7 March 1781, the King's American Regiment was designated the 4th American Regiment and the British Legion, the 5th American Regiment. The British Legion had been formed upon the army's return to New York from Lord Cathcart's Caledonian Volunteers and three other companies. Banastre Tarleton, then an officer in the 79th Regiment of Foot, became the unit's commander. Like the Queen's Rangers, they kept green jackets for their uniform.

As if to mark the 'official recognition' of their abilities, the new 2nd American Regiment celebrated St Patrick's Day by parading, led by their band of music, into the city and forming in front of Lord Rawdon's house. Said the *New York Gazette and Mercury*: 'This single battalion, though only formed a few months ago, marched four hundred strapping fellows, neither influenced by Yankee or Auge; a number, perhaps, equal to all the recruits formed into the rebel army in the same space of time, which shows how easily troops may be formed on this continent. . . .'

The Queen's Rangers had also been active during the winter and spring months. It was not until August that, 'for the first time since they left winter quarters, (they were) permitted to take off their coats, at night, until further orders: in case of sudden alarum, they were ordered to form on their company's parade, undressed, with silence and regularity: the bayonets were never to be unfixed'.

The war, it had been decided, was not to be continued in the northern colonies. They were too rebellious, the country too rough for profitable campaigning. On the other hand, the southern royal governors had strongly expressed their belief that southerners were almost wholly loyal, and would quickly rally to the royal colours and the legal government. Indeed, reports from East and West Florida, which were held by the British, were most encouraging. In one case a group of loyalists from the forts of the Broad and Saluda rivers, the descendants of the Palatines, forced their way from South Carolina, through Georgia, to East Florida. There they formed themselves into two troops of rifle dragoons of forty men each, and four infantry companies of forty-five men each. They took the name of the South Carolina Royalists and chose Colonel Innes, the Provincial Inspector-General, as their colonel. Colonel Thomas Brown raised a ranger band known variously as the King's Rangers, the East Florida Rangers, the Florida Rangers and the Carolina Rangers. This unit reached a strength of some 860 men in all. Moses Kirkland and his Loyal Refugees had been sent from New York to East Florida in 1778 and they were even now raiding into Georgia. In West Florida, where defence was to become more important than attack, the

Major John Small, commander of the 2nd Battalion, Royal Highland Emigrants. The typical military Highland bonnet is stiffened with leather. The plaid is worn over one arm. The collar is unusual, but epaulette, sword, and sword-belt, with a small royal cipher on the end, are typical of Highland units. (McCord Museum, Montreal)

West Florida Royal Foresters and the West Florida Loyalists were forming up.

The plan, then, was to send reinforcements to East Florida. From there they would move quickly north and capture Savannah and all of Georgia. In October 1778 the British Legion, Delancy's Brigade and two battalions of the New Jersey Volunteers were sent to East Florida, along with some regular and Hessian regiments. Savannah quickly fell.

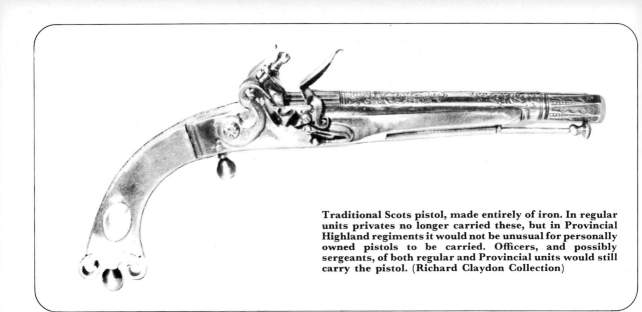

Traditional Scots pistol, made entirely of iron. In regular units privates no longer carried these, but in Provincial Highland regiments it would not be unusual for personally owned pistols to be carried. Officers, and possibly sergeants, of both regular and Provincial units would still carry the pistol. (Richard Claydon Collection)

The rebels could not allow their southernmost capital to remain in British hands, and an allied Continental-French expedition was launched against the city. The city was being held by the original Provincial units, joined by Major James Wright's newly raised Georgia Loyalists, the New York Volunteers, the South Carolina Royalists and the King's Rangers. The enemy armies were unable to make a dent in the city fortifications, and the French were getting anxious to return to the West Indies. A grand assault must be made before the French left. On 9 October 1779 the Allies sprang their attack on the defences, directing their major weight on the Spring Hill redoubt. The South Carolina Royalists were stationed in that particular redoubt, and time and again their well-directed volleys broke up enemy formations. Finally the enemy withdrew, leaving the ground coated with white-coated dead and wounded. Savannah was safe and Georgia returned to the royal fold. Now for South Carolina. While some regiments were marched across by land from Savannah to South Carolina, Sir Henry Clinton brought down reinforcements from New York to assist in the capture of Charleston.

Moving up from the south were the British Legion, the South Carolina Royalists, a battalion of Delancy's Brigade, a battalion of the New Jersey Volunteers, the New York Volunteers and the Georgia Loyalists. With Clinton came several regular and Hessian regiments, the Prince of Wales's American Regiment, the second battalion of the Royal Highland Emigrants, raised in Canada, some of the Guides and Pioneers, the Volunteers of Ireland and the Queen's Rangers.

There had been an abortive attempt to take Charleston by the sea in 1776. This time the lessons had been learned, and the troops were sent to encircle and besiege the city by land. The now mounted British Legion, along with mounted troops of the Queen's Rangers and the three Pennsylvania dragoon companies, closed off the ring and completed the encirclement. The siege began in March, and by 12 May 1780 the Continental Brigadier-General Benjamin Lincoln and his men had had enough. The white flag went up, and the entire southern Continental Army became prisoners. This was the greatest success for British and Provincial arms in the entire war.

Sir Henry returned to New York, leaving Lord Cornwallis to command in the south. As in all previously captured cities, the royal standard was raised and men invited to join Provincial units. Lord Charles Montagu offered rebels taken with the city to serve their King instead of wasting away in prison, and he managed to raise six companies of four officers and ninety-four men each into the Duke of Cumberland's Regiment, which was sent to Jamaica in August 1781 to spend the rest of the war there. The Royal North Carolina Regiment, with red coats faced blue, was raised in the city that spring and eventually boasted 600 men. Lieutenant-Colonel John Hamilton took the unit's command. Two small units, Captain Edward Fenwick's South Carolina Dragoons, with thirty-eight men, and Major John Harrison's South Carolina Rangers, with eighty-one men, were raised. The latter unit remained in the city until it was abandoned in November 1782, whereupon it was sent to St Augustine, East Florida. While not a unit manned by American subjects, Starkloff's Troop of light dragoons was, nevertheless, placed on Provincial muster rolls. The troop was formed by taking men from each of the three Hessian regiments, and they did patrol work around the city until the regiments were returned to New York.

After Charleston's surrender, the 'hero of Saratoga', Horatio Gates, assumed command of a new Continental Army. Lord Cornwallis moved out to meet and destroy him. On 14 August 1780 Gates decided to attack Cornwallis's small army. The British smashed the advance party, and waited as the main rebel army drew into view. They waited on the field and at daybreak Cornwallis formed his troops into one line. The regulars were posted on the right, while the Volunteers of Ireland, the Royal North Carolina Regiment, the British Legion cavalry and two six-pounder and two three-pounder guns were on the left. The North Carolina Refugees and militia were kept in reserve on the right. The rebels attacked all along the line, as at Saratoga. During the attack, which was being held off steadily, Cornwallis spotted a weakness on his enemy's left. He hurled the regulars forward, and they rolled up the rebel line. At that the entire line moved to the attack, and the rebels fled, General Gates far ahead of his troops.

It had been a totally successful, but hard-fought victory. The Volunteers of Ireland lost seventeen privates dead, with another sixty-four wounded, along with three officers, two sergeants and one drummer. Lord Rawdon was so pleased he had silver medals struck and presented to several men who had been particularly heroic.

The south now lay open to Cornwallis, with no appreciable rebel force remaining. He divided his army into three sections. Lord Rawdon was to remain around Charleston, pacifying and holding the country. Major Patrick Ferguson of the

The tin water-canteen used by Provincials came in 'half-moon' and 'kidney' shapes. Holding about one pint, it was plugged with wood and slung on a cord. Canteens were sometimes painted to prevent rusting. (Author's collection)

American Volunteers, who had recovered from wounds received at Brandywine, was to lead troops into the backwoods on a path roughly parallel to Cornwallis who was, himself, to move with the main army north into North Carolina.

Rawdon had his hands full in South Carolina – large rebel army or no large rebel army. His own crack Volunteers of Ireland had so many desertions that in desperation he advertised: 'I will give the inhabitants 10 guineas for the head of any deserter belonging to the Volunteers: and 5 guineas only if they bring him alive. They shall likewise be rewarded though not for that amount for such deserters as they may secure belonging to any other regiment.'

Rawdon's force came to grips with the rebels on 25 April 1781 near Hobkirk's Hill, only a mile from Camden, where they fought a bitter action. His units were the Volunteers of Ireland, the New York Volunteers, the South Carolina Royalists and the Provincial Light Battalion. The latter was made up of various Provincial regimental flank companies. Losses were heavy, and the Volunteers alone lost one officer and twelve other ranks dead, with five officers and seventy other ranks wounded. Despite the desertion orders, sixteen privates and a drummer were missing.

The rebels were again growing in strength and

confidence. All the mounted units having gone with Cornwallis, Rawdon needed cavalry. The people of Charleston rose to the need and 3,000 guineas were collected to arm and accoutre a regiment of dragoons. In June 1781 the South Carolina Royalists were so converted, and they spent the rest of the war mounted.

The town of Ninety Six meanwhile came under siege by one of the rebels' top generals, Nathaniel Greene. Lord Rawdon quickly took the mounted South Carolina Royalists, the New York Volunteers and the Light Battalion, and rushed to the town's relief. Upon his approach Greene abandoned the siege, and Rawdon was able to withdraw the town's garrison to Camden. Another small force, the Prince of Wales's American Regiment and part of the British Legion, were hit at Hanging Rock, S.C., and also forced to withdraw into Camden. Finally Greene felt strong enough to deal with Lord Rawdon's force. On 8 September 1781 he attacked at Eutaw Springs a force made up of a battalion of Delancy's Brigade, two battalions of New Jersey Volunteers, the 2nd Battalion of the Royal Highland Emigrants, the South Carolina Royalists and some mounted New York Volunteers, as well as some regulars.

The defensive line was based on a stone house, and Rawdon deployed his Provincials mainly in the centre. The South Carolina Royalists and New York Volunteers he posted on the left flank. After a volley all along the rebel line, they levelled their bayonets and charged. At first the line held, but the rebels pressed and finally drove the troops out of the stone house. Quickly they reformed some yards away from the house, while a battalion of regular light troops counter-attacked and drove the rebels back to their old position. The rest of the line joined in the attack, and the line was regained.

Both sides claimed victory. The British and Provincials remained on the field that night, but withdrew the next day into Charleston where, with all the troops from the other withdrawn outposts, they remained until the city was finally abandoned in 1782.

General Benedict Arnold

General Horatio Gates

General Nathaniel Greene

King's Mountain

When Lord Cornwallis had split his army into three parts, Major Ferguson had been sent on a line roughly parallel with Cornwallis's. His force included men from his own American Volunteers, a detachment from the Queen's Rangers, the King's American Regiment and the New Jersey Volunteers. As his force advanced further and further into the backwoods, he learned that an overwhelming number of frontiersmen were gathering to fight him. Ferguson quickly withdrew to a perfect defensive position on top of King's Mountain, North Carolina. The ground there was rocky, the hill deeply wooded. It was a fortress ready built.

The mountain men followed, and on the afternoon of 7 October 1780 launched their attack right up the mountain's sides. The Provincials' smoothbore muskets, totally inaccurate beyond fifty yards, were no match for the deadly riflemen from the frontiers. Ferguson himself, riding from position to position rallying his men, was hit by one of the rebel marksmen. As Ferguson's dead body was seen, caught by his stirrup and being dragged about by his crazed charger, his second in command, Captain Abraham de Peyster, had the white flag raised. Any chance of pacifying the backwoods, and returning them to their royal allegiance, was now gone forever.

The war itself had been greatly enlarged. With Burgoyne's fall the French had joined the rebels, followed shortly afterwards by the Spanish. Both European powers had lost badly to Great Britain in the Seven Years War, and ached for revenge. The Spanish began, under the able Governor of Louisiania, Don Bernardo de Galvez, by attempting to take British positions on the Mississippi and in the Floridas, which had been Spanish previously. Reinforcements would have to be sent to these posts, which were being held by handfuls of regulars. It was decided to send the Pennsylvania and Maryland Loyalists from Canada. The Pennsylvania Loyalists, with some 165 effectives, and the Marylanders with 277, were joined by the Waldeck Regiment from Germany. Two West Florida units were formed at the same time.

In the spring of 1779 the reinforcements landed at Pensacola, West Florida's capital, which had some small fortifications and an old stone powder magazine. In March 1780 the Pennsylvanians and Germans were sent to relieve Mobile, then under Spanish siege. After a march of 120 miles through an uninhabited wilderness they found the city had already surrendered, and returned, marching continuously for fourteen days in the process. Shortly after they got back Spanish sails were seen on the horizon, and the small garrison found that they were the next to be besieged. The Loyal American Rangers, who had been recruited in New York in 1780 from among Continental prisoners, were sent from Jamaica to lift the siege. On the way they heard that the city had fallen – it had not – and returned without firing a shot.

Widely issued to Provincial troops under winter conditions, these iron 'ice-creepers' fastened to the shoe with a buckled leather strap. (Author's collection)

Captain Abraham de Peyster, King's American Regiment, who surrendered at King's Mountain after Major Ferguson's death. This interesting primitive painting shows a red coat faced dark blue; the waistcoat appears to be chamois leather. The epaulette and its button are gold, the coat buttons silver and the waistcoat buttons fabric-covered. The overall effect is of rather odd tailoring. (New York Historical Society)

At the end of April 1781 the Spanish, who had left and returned since first arriving, broke ground for a formal siege. An assault was driven off by the city's garrison: the Spanish artillery seemed to be making no appreciable dent in the fortifications: Spanish ammunition was running low. They were considering retiring when an officer from one of the Provincial regiments deserted, bringing the Spanish the information as to the position of the British powder magazine. Immediately they concentrated their fire there, scoring a direct hit. When the smoke had cleared, almost 100 soldiers and sailors lay dead. Despite this setback the garrison held on until 9 May 1781, when Brigadier-General John Campbell, the commanding officer, surrendered. The West

1 North Carolina Militiaman, 1775
2 Private, The King's Royal Regiment of New York, 1777
3 Private, Loyal American Association, 1775

MICHAEL YOUENS

A

1 **Sergeant, Royal Fencible Americans,**
  1776–8
2 **Black Company of Pioneers**
3 **Officer, King's Orange Rangers, 1777**

B

1 Officer, The Prince of Wales's American
Regiment
2 Butler's Rangers
3 Private, Pennsylvania Loyalists,
Philadelphia, 1777

MICHAEL YOUENS

C

1 Highland Company, Queen's Rangers, 1778
2 Hussar Company, Queen's Rangers, 1778
3 Officer, King's American Regiment, 1778

D

1 **Grenadier Sergeant, New Jersey Volunteers, 1778**
2 **Private, Guides and Pioneers, 1779**
3 **Private, Royal Highland Emigrants, 1779**

MICHAEL YOUENS

E

1 Private, 1st Battalion, Jamaica
Rangers, 1780
2 Private, The Newfoundland
Regiment, 1780
3 Private, North Carolina
Highlanders

F

MICHAEL YOUEN

1 **Private, Royal Garrison Regiment, 1783**
2 **Light Infantryman, Loyal American Regiment, 1782**
3 **Private, 3rd Battalion, Delancy's Brigade, 1783**

MICHAEL YOUENS

G

1 Officer, British Legion, 1781
2 Officer, King's American Dragoons, 1782
3 Fifer, New York Volunteers, 1782

H

Florida Loyalist units seem to have been paroled there, while the rest were paroled to New York, where they eventually returned to duty.

Things were not altogether black for British arms. One of the rebels' best generals, the energetic and aggressive Benedict Arnold, had changed sides in an abortive attempt to turn over the rebel stronghold of West Point, above New York City. He immediately organized his own unit, the American Legion, which reached a strength of some 415. Then he launched a series of raids in strength designed to further weaken the already shaken rebel morale, while destroying vital war material. In December 1780 his American Legion, the Guides and Pioneers, the Loyal American Regiment, the Queen's Rangers, the Bucks County Volunteers and the New York Volunteer Rifle Company were landed at Portsmouth, Virginia, to begin a series of raids which would see his men reach as far west as Petersburg and the rebel Governor's home. The troops burned a vital arsenal and forced the Virginia government to flee its capital at Richmond.

While all this was going on, Lord Cornwallis had been moving north. The rebel Gates had been replaced by Nathaniel Greene, whom Cornwallis's army finally met at Guilford Court House. There his regulars and Hessians smashed through the rebel battle lines to victory, but suffered irreplaceable losses in the process. The British Legion, much to its disgust, remained in reserve.

Greene had been moving constantly just in front of Cornwallis. To lighten his load and catch Greene, Cornwallis had the Royal North Carolina Regiment take all his army's wagons back to South Carolina. Now, suffering from his losses at Guilford Court House, and lacking the supplies which had been sent south, Cornwallis felt he had to get out of the Carolinas and into safer Virginia. His other great hope for victory in the Carolinas had been destroyed when Banastre Tarleton, with his British Legion and some regulars, had gone after the rebel, Daniel Morgan.

On 17 January 1781 Morgan had halted, with his back against a river, in a place called Cowpens. Morgan arranged his men in three lines, with militia in front and Continentals in the last line. Tarleton's men came streaming through the first

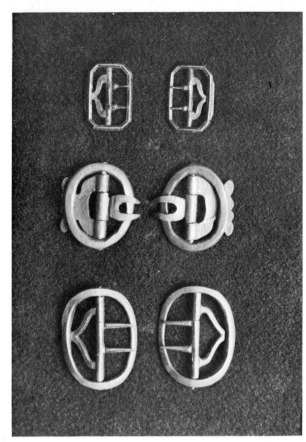

Eighteenth-century knee buckles. Top: Sterling silver buckles, made in England, of the type worn by Provincial officers; centre: crude modern reproduction of rankers' buckles – the originals have insides made of iron, while these are entirely brass; bottom: brass buckles made in Lancaster County, Pennsylvania, of a common labourer's pattern, such as were worn by Provincial rankers. (Author's collection)

lines, the British Legion cavalry striking towards the rear as the militia fled to their left flank. It was then that Morgan launched his own cavalry, which smashed into the British left, crumpling it. Tarleton tried to bring his own mounted men round to meet this attack, but it was all over – the formations had been broken and red-coated regulars and green-coated legionnaires were fleeing the field.

Cornwallis's men said goodbye to the Carolinas; the war was ending in the deep south. Cornwallis arrived in Virginia. (Arnold returned to New York, leaving behind the crack Queen's Rangers. That September he returned to the raiding scene, putting much of New London, Connecticut, to the torch, accompanied by his American Legion and the Loyal American

Regiment.) Opposing Cornwallis in Virginia, while Greene moved further south to regain all the rebel lands, was a small force under Lafayette. This was soon enlarged by the Pennsylvania Line, and the new army was commanded by the German, von Steuben. It fell to the 320-man-strong Queen's Rangers to keep up constant skirmishing in front of the enemy – a duty of which Simcoe reported, 'The incessant marches of the Rangers, and their distance from their stores, had so worn out their shoes that, on Lt. Colonel Simcoe's calling for a return, it appeared that near fifty men were absolutely barefooted. . . .' None the less, the Queen's Rangers had been newly clothed and accoutred just prior to the campaign. The regiment, Simcoe said, '. . . had substituted light caps, neat and commodius, in room of the miserable contract hats, which had been sent from England'. In those caps were worn black and white feathers, a sign of mourning for Major André, hanged by the rebels as a spy.

Major-General John Burgoyne

Lord Cornwallis

Plain brass cartridge-box plate with engraved royal cipher. General-purpose plates like this were common among Provincial units, while regulars often had special regimentally marked plates. Examples like this have been found at Ticonderoga, and on the sites of British Army camps around New York. (Author's collection)

Baron von Steuben

Slowly Cornwallis's force continued its withdrawal, ending at the small town of Yorktown. It was there Washington saw his chance. Leaving a token force to oppose the New York garrison, he hurried his main army down to the small, sleepy southern town. At the same time, the French Navy had defeated the Royal Navy in the bay off Yorktown, and British superiority at sea was temporarily ended. The noose was knotted, and a formal siege was begun. Cornwallis launched a sortie across the river in an attempt to move his troops to safety, to be led by the Queen's Rangers. A fierce storm blew up, however, and it was impossible to ferry the men across the raging river. It was now only a matter of time. Sir Henry Clinton, in New York, felt too threatened to send reinforcements until too late. On 18 October 1781 Lord Cornwallis's army, including the Queen's Rangers and a handful of other Provincials including some from the New Jersey Volunteers, surrendered their arms.

The war in America was virtually over.

The Bitter End

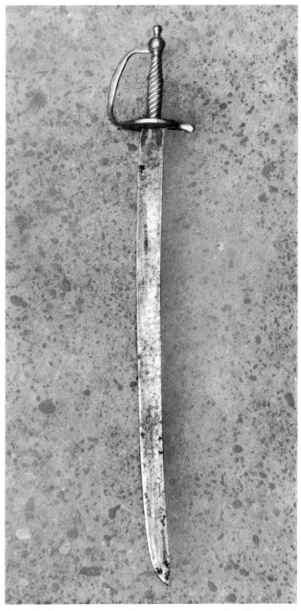

So-called 1742-pattern hanger, as worn by Provincial sergeants and grenadiers. There are many variations, but this brass-hilted example may be considered the classic type. The blade length is 58.5 centimetres. (Crisman Collection)

For the Provincial troops there was still action ahead. In February 1780 Governor Dalling of Jamaica gathered a force of the Jamaica Legion, the Jamaica Volunteers and the Royal Batteaux men. He struck the Spanish first in Honduras, then moved to capture Fort St John in Nicaragua. Although the capture was virtually bloodless, maintaining the fort brought with it diseases, and the little force lost men by the dozens. Dalling finally simply abandoned it and withdrew to Jamaica.

In August 1782 Major William Odell's Loyal American Rangers successfully raided the Spanish post at Black River, Honduras. Besides Odell's own regiment there were some 500 Negroes and 600 Mesquite Indians. The raid ended with the capture of the Spanish Army's entire Guatemala Regiment of 742 men, who were sent to Omoa,

Regimental coat of William Jarvis, a captain in the Queen's Rangers. The tall 'rise and fall' collar, introduced about 1791, indicates that this coat was probably worn during Jarvis's service between 1781 and 1802. However, the general cut, lace and colours are probably identical to those of the period 1775–83. The silver lace is embroidered in an odd 'tear-drop' design, but the chevron lacing at the cuff, and the two epaulettes, are typical of mounted officers of the period. (Collections of the Toronto Historical Board at Historical Fort, York, Toronto)

Epaulette detail on the Jarvis coat. Typical of Provincial officers, this example has lace or embroidery of metallic thread laid on an epaulette of facing colour. Solid metallic lace epaulettes, often with 'pips', thistles or crowns, were also widely used. (Toronto Historical Board)

Tail decoration on the Jarvis coat. The tails are permanently turned back by fastening with a piece of regimental facing cloth embroidered with a crown and wreath design. Other styles of the period included, for officers, brass hearts pinned to each tail and fastened together; hearts or similar shapes cut from facing cloth and sewn to each tail, concealing a hook-and-eye fastening; or simply hooks and eyes placed between the coat and lining. Other ranks often used a piece of regimental lace, sewn over red cloth and with a central button, to hold back the tails. Note the 'raw' or unhemmed outer edges, typical of British and Provincial military coats of the period. (Toronto Historical Board)

Honduras, as prisoners of war, 'much to the displeasure of negroes & Indians'.

There was still action around New York. New Provincial regiments continued to be raised. An advertisement in an April 1782 copy of the city's *Royal Gazette* called for 'likely and spirited young lads desirous of serving their King and country and who prefer riding to going on foot'. Volunteers were offered ten guineas on their enlistment. The unit was the King's American Dragoons, then being raised by Lieutenant-Colonel Benjamin Thompson, later to become famous as Count Rumford. This new unit was completed with members of the Queen's Rangers and the British Legion who had been left in the city, as well as the Volunteers of New England, Stewart's Provincial Dragoons and various other small units.

Prince William Henry, then a Royal Navy midshipman, visited the city when his ship docked there that August, and inspected the King's American Dragoons. According to Colonel Thompson, the Prince '. . . might have easily mistaken us for an established British Regiment of Light Dragoons'. Thompson was so pleased that he said he 'would not be ashamed to show the regiment in Hyde Park'. During the inspection His Highness presented the regiment its colours, in a typical Provincial colours presentation ceremony. The regiment marched before the Prince, performing a marching salute. Then they returned, dismounted and formed a semicircle in front of the reviewing canopy. The regimental chaplain delivered 'an appropriate address', after which the men took off their helmets, laid down their weapons, raised their right arms and took an oath of fidelity. After the chaplain's benediction, Thompson received the colours from the Prince, and passed them to the two eldest cornets. There were three cheers; the band played 'God Save the King', the guns fired a royal salute and the ceremony was over.

After such a fancy send-off, it would be nice to report some stirring victories for the King's American Dragoons. Alas, they merely served in some local skirmishes until disbanded a year later.

Provincial units were generally growing smaller, both through battle losses and desertions. On 21 May 1782 the new Commander-in-Chief, General Sir Guy Carleton, reviewed the King's

Engraved brass sword-belt plate of the King's American Dragoons. (Rebecca Katcher)

American Dragoons, the American Legion, the Queen's Legion, the British Legion and the Loyal American Regiment. He said that he was 'extremely well satisfied; [but] since the provincial corps were so weak, however, the commanders were asked to look around diligently for recruits and send in without delay detailed accounts of the recruiting money received, how it was spent, and who received rations. This, [said the Hessian Adjutant-General], will cause much explanation. Later exact and detailed specifications were drawn up as to who is entitled to receive rations and who not. In order to prevent dishonesty, the receipts are countersigned in the districts where the troops are stationed.'

The Provincials' final action came in April 1783 when Major Andrew DeVeaux, from South Carolina, led a small Provincial band from St Augustine to New Providence, the most important island of the Bahamas. The islands had fallen to

Engraved brass officer's sword-belt plate of Butler's Rangers. (Rebecca Katcher)

Cartridge-box plate of Butler's Rangers. This seems to be the regular cast brass plate of the type issued to regiments which had no particular unit design; the words 'Butler's Rangers' have been engraved later. (Rebecca Katcher)

the Spanish the year before, and in a daring bloodless bluff, the Provincials coolly retook them.

In October 1782 word reached America that Great Britain would recognize American independence.

'You cannot conceive [wrote Colonel Thompson to an English friend], nor can any language describe the Distress that all ranks of people here have been thrown into by the intelligence of the Independence of America being acknowledged by Great Britain, and the loyalists being given up to the Mercy of their Enemies. The Militia who have for some weeks done the whole of the Garrison duty in this City have premtory refused to serve any longer, and the General has been obliged to relieve them by bringing regular

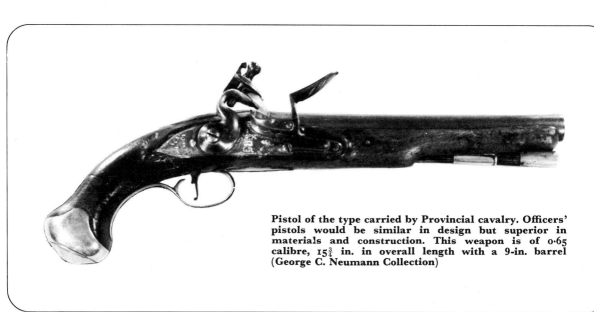

Pistol of the type carried by Provincial cavalry. Officers' pistols would be similar in design but superior in materials and construction. This weapon is of 0·65 calibre, $15\frac{3}{4}$ in. in overall length with a 9-in. barrel (George C. Neumann Collection)

Regimental buttons of a selection of Provincial units. Top, left to right: the Queen's Rangers, 2nd American Regiment, the New York Volunteers, the King's Regiment; bottom, left to right: King's Royal Regiment of New York, Butler's Rangers, King's Orange Rangers, Royal Highland Emigrants, the King's American Dragoons. (Rebecca Katcher)

Troops into Town. The Loyalists at Lloyds Neck and the other posts are in a state of Anarchy and confusion little short of actual rebellion. Papers have been struck up about town, inviting Sir Guy Carleton to take command of the Army here and oppose by force the measures of the New Administration and promising thousands to assist him. . . . The Provincial Corps will disband of themselves or . . . they will take arms in opposition to these measures.'

Certain Provincial regiments were in a different class, however, as they had already been taken on the British, or regular, establishment. They included the Royal Highland Emigrants, now the 84th Regiment of Foot; the Volunteers of Ireland, now the 105th Regiment of Foot; the British Legion; the Queen's Rangers; the King's American Regiment; and the Royal Garrison Regiment. The latter unit had been formed in New York in September 1778 from men of other regiments unable, because of wounds or disease, to perform active duty. They had served in garrison duties in New York and Bermuda.

In March 1783 the Hessian Adjutant-General reported:

'The provincials have been notified that they must expect some reduction. For this purpose every battalion has been ordered to prepare its rolls into columns, showing, from the first officer to the last man, whether they want to escape this reduction, or be transported to Nova Scotia without expense to themselves, or, lastly, return to their former homes with three months pay. The established provincial officers are excluded from this arrangement and will receive half pay.'

Later, in August, he wrote:

'Those who wish to remain in America have been ordered to draw pay until the 25th of October, and two weeks' maintenance and have been told to cross the lines in groups of three. Only a few have chosen to remain in America. Most of them desire to go to Nova Scotia, wither the provincial corps noted below will be transported as units and where they will disband. None of them have been offered passage to England. The units are: Garrison Battalion, whose 1st Battalion is in the Bermudas; New York Volunteers; New Jersey Volunteers, all three battalions; Delancy's Brigade, 1st and 2nd Battalions; The Prince of Wales's American Regiment; Pennsylvania Loyalists; Maryland Loyalists; Guides and Pioneers.'

Two privates of the New Jersey Volunteers did try to return to their homes in Sussex County, New Jersey, where they were badly beaten by

A British caricature of an American rifleman. (Metropolitan Museum of Art)

on a regular basis has been put at between 30,000 and 50,000. In 1780, when Washington's army numbered some 9,000, the Provincial Corps had some 8,000 in its ranks. There were 312 companies commissioned throughout the war.

Why, then, did they not win? They were at first ignored. When finally accepted they never fully won the confidence of their British comrades in arms. A South Carolina loyalist, Colonel Robert Gray, wrote: 'almost every British officer regarded with contempt and indifference the establishment of a militia among a people differing so much in customs and manners from themselves'. An intelligent regular subaltern recorded that he felt Provincial troops were '. . . not remarkable for rallying, the first check they receive ensures victory over them'. It was only the work of Provincials which kept Cornwallis's wagons moving in North Carolina. And yet, a period historian recorded shortly after the war: 'In return for the exertions, the militia were maltreated, by abusive language, and even beaten by some officers in the quarter-master general's department.' A British claims commissioner after the war sneeringly commented on the petition of a former New Jersey Volunteers officer: 'It has been his Misfortune that the Troubles put him for a time into the situation of a Gentleman.' The officer had been a tavern-keeper.

Edward Winslow constantly complained about lack of British support. The Provincials, he wrote at one point, 'if duly encouraged would have been much more respectable in point of numbers than they are at present'.

The loyalists were also, at heart, Americans. Major Walter Dulany wrote Sir Guy Carleton on 29 March 1783:

'My duty as a subject; the happiness which America enjoyed under the British government; and the miseries to which she would be reduced by an independence were the motives that induced me to join the British Army; nor are there any dangers, or difficulties that I would not cheerfully undergo, to effect a happy restoration.

'But at the same time, that I acted, with the greatest zeal against my rebellious countrymen I never forgot that I was an American – if therefore, Sir, Independance should be granted and the war still continued, I should deem it

their former neighbours. Another member of the regiment was killed while visiting his parents in Morris County, New Jersey, by the 'lovers of liberty'.

Besides their pay, the men who chose Nova Scotia received land grants. New Brunswick, Canada, was largely settled in 1783 by men from the Queen's Rangers, King's American Regiment, New York Volunteers, Loyal American Regiment, two battalions of Delancy's Brigade, three battalions of the New Jersey Volunteers, the Prince of Wales's American Regiment, the Maryland and Pennsylvania Loyalists, the American Legion, the British Legion and the Guides and Pioneers. The garrison battalion, because of the men's poor health, was disbanded in England where the climate was better than Nova Scotia.

The war was over.

As a whole, the number of loyalists who fought

These pictures of a reproduction loyalist uniform and
field equipment, made from original patterns and care-
fully matched materials, give an impression of a soldier's
appearance in the late eighteenth century

Reproduction of eighteenth-century 'small-clothes', made to original patterns, and showing the characteristic tightly tailored legs and full seat of the breeches, and the long, puffed shirtsleeves. These garments are typical of all nationalities of the period. (Author's collection)

extremely improper to remain in a situation, obliging me to act either directly or indirectly against Americans.'

There was, too, great pressure put on loyalists from their 'patriotic' neighbours. On 6 June 1783 a Phebe Ward wrote her husband Edmund, serving in a Provincial unit:

'Kind Husband, I am sorry to aquant you that our farme is sold . . . thay said if I did not quitt posesion that they had aright to take any think on the farme or in the house to pay the Cost of a law sute and imprisen me I have sufered most Every thing but death it self in your long absens pray Grant me spedy Releaf or God only knows what will become of me and my frendles Children . . .

'Thay say my posesion was nothing youre husband has forfeted his estate by joining the British Enemy with a free and vollentary will and thereby was forfeted to the Stat and sold.

'All at present from you cind and loveing Wife.'

The Continentals hated the Provincials with that special bitterness which a civil war engenders. A captured rebel sailor recalled:

'The Refugees, or Royalists as they termed themselves, were viewed by us with scorn and hatred. I do not recollect, however, that a guard of these miscreants was placed over us more than three times, during which their presence occasioned much tumult and confusion; for the prisoners could not endure the sight of these men, and occasionally assailed them with abusive language: while they in return treated us with all the severity in their power.

'They never answered any of our remarks respecting them; but would merely point to their uniforms, as if saying, We are clothed by our Sovereign, while you are naked. They were as much gratified at the idea of leaving us, as we were at seeing them depart. Many provoking gestures were made by the prisoners as they left the ship, and our curses followed them as far as we could make ourselves heard.'

The Plates

A1 North Carolina Militiaman, 1775

The militia which was defeated at Moore's Creek, North Carolina, were not uniformed in any sense of the word. One of their number recorded wearing a long hunting shirt, a garment generally made of white linen like a fringed farmer's smock, and buckskin breeches. This private wears a black slouch hat, and his accoutrements consist of a powder-horn and bullet-bag only. His weapon is a long fowler, made not unlike a military weapon but designed principally for hunting birds.

A2 Private, The King's Royal Regiment of New York, 1777

Also known as 'Johnson's Royal Greens', this was one of the first well-equipped Provincial units. The regiment served in a number of engagements in upper New York state, and was finally disbanded in Canada in June 1784. There were two battalions, with a total of more than 1,290 men of all ranks. Originally they wore green coats, probably with predominantly blue facings; however, Provincials took any coats which were issued, and it is possible that red and white facings were also worn by some in the regiment. In 1778 the regiment drew red coats with blue facings, in which they finished the war. Accoutrements and arms were of the standard British patterns, including the Long Land model musket usually issued to Provincials.

A3 Private, Loyal American Association, 1775

It was not until 1776 that Provincial troops were uniformed. This member of the Loyal American Association, illustrated as he would have appeared while in Boston during the siege, wears his civilian suit and a white scarf tied round his arm as a field-sign. His accoutrements are obsolete British Army issue, and he carries a Long Land model 'Brown Bess' musket with wooden ramrod.

B1 Sergeant, Royal Fencible Americans, 1776–8

This unit was raised in Nova Scotia in June 1775, from Europeans and rebel deserters. Numbering only about 460 men of all ranks, the unit remained in Nova Scotia until disbanded in 1783. Originally they wore green coats faced white, as here; but in 1778 they changed to red coats faced blue. The sergeant is distinguished by plain white lace bound round his buttonholes, a scarlet worsted sash with a central white stripe, silver hat lace

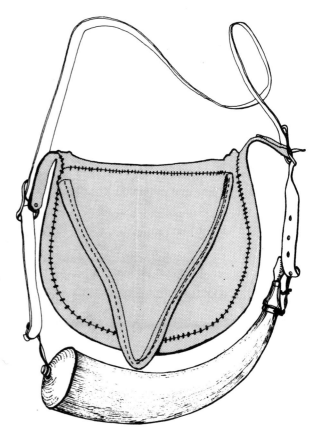

A hunting bag with attached powder-horn. Used for preference by riflemen, only in the absence of cartridges by musketeers, owing to the different loading techniques

and a short sword or hanger – the regulation insignia of a British sergeant of the day.

B2 Black Company of Pioneers

In Philadelphia it was decided that a pioneer company was needed to build the fortifications, keep the streets clear and work on the dock. A Negro unit was raised to perform these tasks. Each man was issued a greatcoat for winter wear, a hat, a green sailor's jacket, a white shirt and winter trousers. The winter trousers then in use by the British Army tended to be form-fitting gaiter trousers of red, blue or brown wool.

B3 Officer, King's Orange Rangers, 1777

This unit was raised in New York in December 1776 as a mounted rifle company. The 'Orange' referred to their place of recruitment – Orange County, New York – as well as to their facings. It was a difficult colour to produce with the dyes of the period, and the actual shade varied widely between yellow and brownish red. Officers' coats would be cut from better material than those of other ranks. The silver metal decreed for this corps appears as hat lace, coat lace and buttons, gorget and sword hilt. The officer's sash is of crimson silk. The officer illustrated wears boots for riding, and uses a mounted man's sword.

C1 Officer, The Prince of Wales's American Regiment

This unit, which eventually mustered 610 men, mostly from Connecticut, was described by a British officer on its arrival at Newport, Rhode Island: 'They appear to be a very good body of men and are well Clothed and Armed. They are provided with new Camp Equipage.' An original officer's coat survives to this day; it is of scarlet cloth faced dark blue, and the faded copper buttons and metallic lace still bear traces of gilding. As with many Provincial units, some men of the regiment seem to have worn green facings as well as the regulation blue.

C2 Butler's Rangers

One of the most effective of all Provincial units, Butler's Rangers were recruited along the New York–Canada border in 1777–8. By December

A selection of (top) halberds; (bottom) spontoons

Sketch of 1773-pattern light dragoon sabre, issued to Provincial mounted troops. With either a brass or an iron hilt, the blade was 3 feet long. (Rebecca Katcher)

1778 they had six companies; eventually the strength rose to ten companies, and two light field-pieces. They were disbanded in Canada in June 1784. The uniform consisted of a light infantry-man's leather cap with a brass front-plate, green jacket and white linen gaiter trousers. Leather belts were black, and officers had engraved brass pelt-plates on their sword-belts. Most of the men carried the 'Brown Bess', but the famous Penn-sylvania rifle was probably much in evidence as well.

C3 Private, Pennsylvania Loyalists, Philadelphia, 1777
This battalion, of three companies, was raised in Philadelphia in 1777; the uniform was virtually identical to that of the British regular, and was typical of the majority of Provincial units. The red coats were faced olive-green, and white linen or duck trousers were worn in the summer. The regimental lace had an interwoven design, like that of the regulars, but Provincial lace patterns are no longer known. The distinctions of officers were in gold metal.

D1 Highland Company, Queen's Rangers, 1778
While in Philadelphia the Queen's Rangers recruited a Highland Company, dressed in tradi-tional costume; they seem to have worn the usual green jacket of their corps, without lapels. The bonnet was the small, Lowland type, and the kilts were of the government sett used in all army-issue kilts, and known today as the 'Black Watch plaid'. They wore sporrans, cartridge-boxes, dirks and bayonets.

D2 Hussar Company, Queen's Rangers, 1778
Although originally a foot unit, the Queen's Rangers were later augmented by mounted troops. At first the mounted men seem to have worn cocked hats; however, after a trooper had

been shot in mistake for a rebel, the hussar head-dress shown here was adopted. The silver crescent badge was often engraved; one example has been found with the name 'Monmouth', a personal battle-honour. The accoutrements were standard British dragoon issue, except that black leather was used in place of whitened buff.

D3 Officer, King's American Regiment, 1778
One of the finest of the Provincial units, the regiment was designated 4th American Regiment in 1781, and taken on the British regular establish-ment the following year. It seems that they referred to themselves as the 110th Regiment of Foot. The red coats were faced dark blue, and the officers wore gold metal. Specially engraved gorgets and belt-plates of officers still survive; the regiment seems to have been one of the better-dressed units. The strength is recorded at 833 men. The regi-ment fought at Fort Clinton and Fort Mont-gomery, at Newport, at King's Mountain, and on raids in Virginia, Georgia, and East Florida.

E1 Grenadier Sergeant, New Jersey Volunteers, 1778
With an eventual strength of six battalions, this was the largest single Provincial regiment raised. Originally dressed in green coats, the unit received red faced blue in 1778. The buttons of the first three battalions were arranged evenly, in pairs or in threes, according to the battalion. Officers wore silver metal. Many Provincial units followed British regular practice and raised both light and grenadier companies within the battalion. This grenadier wears a typical bearskin cap, and is further distinguished by a brass match-case on his cartridge-box sling.

E2 Private, Guides and Pioneers, 1779
This unit was raised with the Loyal American Regiment, and served largely with them. Like

their regular British counterparts they wore short brick-red jackets with black cuffs and collars, and no lapels. The white linen gaiter trousers would have been convenient working dress.

E3 Private, Royal Highland Emigrants, 1779

The Royal Highland Emigrants were raised in Canada, recruiting among discharged veterans of regular Highland regiments of the Seven Years War and their families. Two battalions were raised, and the unit was taken on the British regular establishment in January 1779, as the 84th Regiment of Foot. The men wore typical Highland uniform with blue facings, and lace consisted of a blue stripe between two red stripes. Officers used gold metal.

F1 Private, 1st Battalion, Jamaica Rangers, 1780

This Negro corps was raised in the summer of 1779, and eventually mustered three battalions.

They wore plain white coats with red facings, and standard British Army small-clothes and equipment.

F2 Private, The Newfoundland Regiment, 1780

Raised in that year, the Newfoundland Regiment was placed on the British regular establishment on 25 December 1782. They were issued with blue coats faced red, originally intended for Royal Artillery troops at Gibraltar. The lace was plain white, however, and the pewter buttons bore the word 'Newfoundland'. The regiment saw no action, and was disbanded in 1783.

F3 Private, North Carolina Highlanders

When Lord Cornwallis moved into North Carolina the colony's royal Governor, Joseph Martin, raised the royal standard and called for the Scots communities in the back country to join his forces. He issued his Highlanders short blue jackets, and

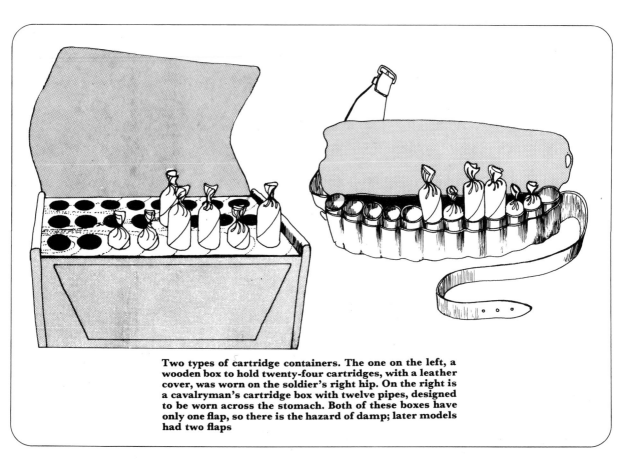

Two types of cartridge containers. The one on the left, a wooden box to hold twenty-four cartridges, with a leather cover, was worn on the soldier's right hip. On the right is a cavalryman's cartridge box with twelve pipes, designed to be worn across the stomach. Both of these boxes have only one flap, so there is the hazard of damp; later models had two flaps

Highland kilts borrowed from the stores of the 1st Foot. The accoutrements were standard issue, but unlike regular Highland regiments the volunteers probably kept their broadswords as well as their muskets. The unit numbered 611 men.

G1 Private, Royal Garrison Regiment, 1783
This unit was formed from men of other regiments whose physical disabilities ruled out more active service. Red coats with both blue and green facings seem to have been issued. The regiment's one battle was the defence of Paulus Hook, New Jersey, on 18–19 August 1779. At one stage a battalion was sent to Bermuda. Unlike other Provincial units, the men were allowed to return to England on disbandment, rather than being obliged to face the harsh Canadian winter.

G2 Light Infantryman, Loyal American Regiment, 1782
Besides grenadier companies, Provincial regiments often had light companies; these were frequently brought together in a separate 'light battalion'. Typical uniform features of the light troops were the leather cap; a short coat, like a cropped regulation coat; and a red waistcoat. The cap was of boiled leather, with three chains sewn round it and a front-plate with a painted regimental design. Feathers were often worn in the cap. This regiment was raised in 1776 and served throughout the war; at one time or another it seems to have worn both buff and green facings, not uncommon among Provincials.

G3 Private, 3rd Battalion, Delancy's Brigade, 1783
This brigade, made up of three battalions, was one of the first Provincial corps raised in New York. Winter dress included wool gaiter trousers in red, blue or brown. The buttons were worn evenly spaced, in pairs or in threes, according to the battalion number.

H1 Officer, British Legion, 1781
The title 'British Legion' once had far more sinister connotations than it does today! A British officer, Banastre Tarleton, was given command of this unit, which had been created from several

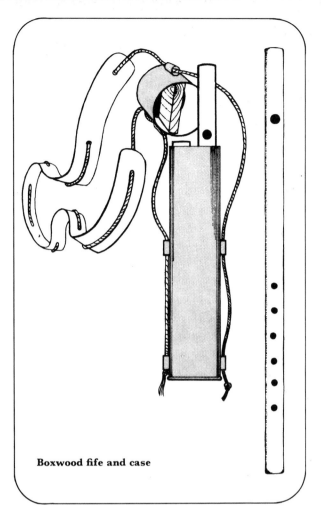

Boxwood fife and case

independent companies in New York in 1778. It served mainly in the south, and in that part of the country 'Tarleton's Quarter' – i.e. a policy of no prisoners taken – became a hated phrase. (Tarleton was to attract attention years later when, as a Westminster M.P., he led a faction bitterly opposed to Wellington.) His Legion wore dragoon helmets, green jackets, and standard dragoon accoutrements; in the summer their campaign dress consisted of white smocks or white-sleeved waistcoats. They were taken on to the American establishment as the 5th American Regiment, and, in 1782, on to the British regular establishment as 'a regiment of horse'.

H2 Officer, King's American Dragoons, 1782
This was one of the last Provincial regiments raised, created from six independent New York

companies and detachments from units interned at Yorktown. It was a light dragoon unit, created strictly along regular lines, and wearing red coats faced blue and dragoon helmets. Officers wore gold metal. Their horses were sold off in New York and the regiment was disbanded at Halifax, Nova Scotia, in April 1783.

H3 Fifer, New York Volunteers, 1782

The coats of Provincial musicians, like those of regulars, were in the reverse of the regimental colours. Their caps were like those of grenadiers often with designs of drums and flags on the front plate in place of grenadier insignia. The fifer carried his two instruments in a brass fife-case slung on his right side by cords of different colours, woven through a whitened buff leather shoulder-belt. The brass case itself was often engraved with the royal arms. This musician's regiment was raised in 1776 and served in both northern and southern theatres. On 2 May 1779 it was redesignated the 3rd American Regiment.